Foreword III

Preface V

Introduction VII

The Foundations of our Compound Republic 1

The Rights, Powers and Duties of State Legislatures 13

The Constitutional Line 23

Therefore, What ... ? 33

Appendices 41

Index 55

Foreword

STATE OF UTAH
OFFICE OF THE GOVERNOR
SALT LAKE CITY, UTAH
84114-2220

GARY R. HERBERT
GOVERNOR

GREG BELL
LIEUTENANT GOVERNOR

Foreword: "Where's the Line?"

I have had the distinct honor, twice as the Governor of the State of Utah and twice as its Lieutenant Governor, to swear an oath to "support, obey and defend" the Constitution of the United States and the Constitution of the State of Utah, as prescribed in Article VI and Article IV, respectively, of those sacred documents.

I also swore that I would "discharge the duties of my office with fidelity." I appreciate the use of the word fidelity, defined as "faithfulness, loyalty, strict conformity to truth or fact, and exact correspondence to the original." It is my responsibility as an executive officer of a sovereign state to ensure that the Constitution of our nation, and the Constitution of my state, are followed *with fidelity*.

Today, we find ourselves in dire circumstances whereby words like faithfulness, loyalty, conformity, and exactness are not only imprecise in describing the federal government's adherence to the national Constitution, they are simply counterfactual. That the federal government should be constrained by the "few and defined" powers enumerated to it by the Constitution seems today a quaint notion from a simpler time when men wore breeches and Congress had nine full-time employees, four of whom were chaplains.

Recognizing the propensity of all governments to amass power unto themselves, the Founding Fathers designed a system whereby the federal government would not only be checked by internal separations of power, but by external ones. Namely, the people and the states, unto whom all powers *not* delegated to the federal government *are* amassed.

The states, then, serve as a vital bulwark against federal overreach, and the diminution of our liberties and inalienable rights which results. As Alexander Hamilton stated, "This balance between the National and State governments…is of the utmost importance. It forms a double security to the people."

It is the sworn responsibility of state officeholders to ensure that the fortifications of federalism – the states – do not stand idly by as the federal government usurps power and authority which is not reserved to it. The states are not powerless agents of federal authority, and they must not comport themselves as such.

Foreword

In his timely and constructive pamphlet, Representative Ken Ivory illuminates what the proper "line" of separation between the states and the federal government should be, and outlines steps the states can take to discharge their duty to maintain it. He does this by drawing chiefly from the text of the Constitution itself, and on contemporaneous words of the Founding Fathers who wrote it and who give first-hand insight to their intent.

The Constitution of the United States is the greatest governing document which has ever been devised and is our country's most important contribution to history and humankind. It is more than deserving of our efforts to ensure *fidelity* to it.

Gary R. Herbert

Gary R. Herbert
Governor
State of Utah

Preface

The Founders knew from brutal experience that the kind of government being promoted by the British ministry—a unitary form operating under an unwritten (or "living") constitution—would hamper the cause of freedom and human happiness. Accordingly, the Founders, with the consent of the American people, decided that our Constitution would be in writing, and would divide power between central and state governments. Under this written Constitution, the three branches of the federal government received important, but limited, powers. All other authority was reserved to the states and the people.

The Constitution is not a mere list of recommendations to be followed if convenient; *it is the law*. In fact, it is the supreme law. All state and federal lawmakers and officers take office at least partly by reason of it, and all are required to swear an oath to support it. Officials who fail to honor that oath thereby deny their own legitimacy. As leading Founders recognized, all serving under the Constitution are duty-bound to defend its divisions of authority. State lawmakers and officials in particular do not merely have the right to guard against federal encroachment; *they are legally and morally obligated to do so.*

As the federal government has metastasized in defiance of all constitutional limits, many state officials—aware of their sworn duty to arise and defend, but conscious of their own responsibility to remain within constitutional limits—have wrestled with the question: "Where's the line?" In this deftly executed pamphlet, Representative Ken Ivory answers that question, summarizing for other state officials the line as the Constitution draws it, or, more precisely, as the Founders themselves did—for Representative Ivory has ensured that most of this pamphlet is written by them.

– Robert G. Natelson
    Senior Fellow in Constitutional Jurisprudence
    The Independence Institute

Introduction

Upon being elected to the Utah House of Representatives, I realized that, as a *state legislator*, I would raise my hand and swear an oath under Article VI to uphold and defend the Constitution of the United States (in addition to swearing an oath to uphold and defend the Utah Constitution).

As an oath-bound member of a state legislature, I felt compelled to know:
- What are the constitutional rights and powers of state legislatures?
- What is the constitutional responsibility of a state legislature?
- Where exactly is the line between the jurisdiction of the several states and that of the federal government?

In establishing a new kind of nation, certain "self-evident," fundamental principles guided the revolutionary work of the Founders:

1. It is the nature and disposition of men and governments to amass unbridled power,
2. Man's unalienable rights come only from the Creator (not from a government or a court), and
3. Governmental powers come only from the people (not from a government or a court).

By means of a written constitution, the Founders deliberately designed a *compound republic*, whereby the powers delegated by the People were divided between the states and the federal government so that *"the different governments will control each other."* In addition to the internal check of the separation of powers among the three branches of the federal government, the states are by design the critical external check on federal government power. The Founders engineered the Constitution in this manner to specifically create *"a double security to the rights of the People."* (James Madison, Federalist 51, 1788) (emphasis added)

The people charged the state legislatures with the constitutional responsibility to *"erect barriers at the constitutional line as cannot be surmounted either by themselves or by the General Government."* (Thomas Jefferson, Letter to Archibald Stewart, 1791) (emphasis added)

This careful division of powers between the states and the federal government, and the external constitutional controls over the power of each, were not established merely for the sake of state power and jurisdiction. They were established to preserve and maintain the compound republic itself in order to secure the rights of the people.

John Dickinson, a major Founder too little recognized today, wrote that *"It will be their own FAULTS, if the several States suffer the federal sovereignty to interfere in the things of their respective jurisdictions."* George Washington wholly endorsed this statement.

The Founders who devised this deliberate network of constitutional checks and balances clearly intended that the state legislatures be constitutionally duty-bound to:

> ... jealously and closely watch the operations of this Government, and BE ABLE TO RESIST WITH MORE EFFECT EVERY ASSUMPTION OF POWER, [BETTER] THAN ANY OTHER POWER ON EARTH CAN DO ... [as the] sure guardians of the people's liberty.
> – James Madison, Introduction of the Bill of Rights, The Annals of Congress, House of Representatives, First Congress, 1st Session, 448-460, 1789 (emphasis added)

My own state constitution, like the constitutions of some other states, provides that *"Frequent recurrence to fundamental principles*[1] *is essential to the security of individual rights and the perpetuity of free government."* (Utah Constitution, Article 1, Section 27)

How can we expect to enjoy the blessings of liberty, peace, and prosperity secured by our Constitution if we fail to fully appreciate or if we allow ourselves to stray from its fundamental principles? In a day when the federal government appears intent upon exercising unbounded power over virtually every aspect of Americans' daily lives, state legislatures, state legislators, and their constituents need to *"recur to fundamental principles"* by frequently asking the question:

"Where's the Line, America?"

---

[1] "No free government, or the blessings of liberty, can be preserved to any people but by a firm adherence to justice, moderation, temperance, frugality, and virtue; and by a frequent recurrence to fundamental principles." – George Mason, Virginia Convention of Delegates, 1776

THE FOUNDATIONS OF OUR COMPOUND REPUBLIC

THE FOUNDERS OF THIS NATION UNDERSTOOD THAT IT IS THE NATURE AND DISPOSITION OF MEN AND GOVERNMENTS TO AMASS AND CONSOLIDATE UNBRIDLED POWER AND CONTROL—RESULTING IN WHAT THEY CALLED "TYRANNY."

Our constitutional system of government (which many of the Founders called a miracle), created a network of *internal* and *external checks and balances* as defenses against the consolidation of government power. This was the product of the Founders' personal experience and their deep historical understanding that (as Lord Acton was to say at a later time) "power corrupts; absolute power corrupts absolutely."

In 8th grade Civics class, most of us learned about the *internal checks*—the "separation of powers"—among the three branches of the federal government.

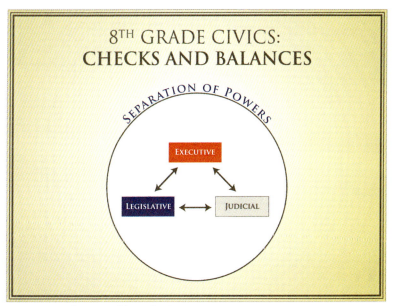

Separation of Powers of the Federal Government

> *A JUST ESTIMATE OF THAT LOVE OF POWER, AND PRONENESS TO ABUSE IT, WHICH PREDOMINATES IN THE HUMAN HEART IS SUFFICIENT TO SATISFY US OF THE TRUTH OF THIS POSITION. THE NECESSITY OF RECIPROCAL CHECKS IN THE EXERCISE OF POLITICAL POWER ... HAS BEEN EVINCED BY EXPERIMENTS ANCIENT AND MODERN.*
> – George Washington, Farewell Address, 1796 (emphasis added)

> The use of checks and balances in the forms of government is to create delays and multiply diversities of interests, by which the tendency on a sudden to violate them may be counteracted.
> – John Adams, Thoughts on Government, 1776

However, it is likely that your Civics class (or your university-level American History class for that matter) gave only passing reference, at best, to the ***external controls*** that state legislatures are under constitutional oath to exert so as to curb federal abuses of power.

> When all government, domestic and foreign, in little as in great things, shall be drawn to Washington as the center of all power, *IT WILL RENDER POWERLESS THE CHECKS PROVIDED OF ONE GOVERNMENT ON ANOTHER*, and will become as venal and oppressive as the government from which we separated.
> – Thomas Jefferson, Letter to Charles Hammond, 1821 (emphasis added)

Here are some of the other statements the Founders made on the subject:

> If men were angels, no government would be necessary. If angels were to govern men, neither *EXTERNAL* nor *INTERNAL CONTROLS ON GOVERNMENT* would be necessary.
> – James Madison, Federalist 51, 1788 (emphasis added)

> What has destroyed liberty and the rights of man in every government which has ever existed under the sun? The generalizing and concentrating all cares and powers into one body, no matter whether of the autocrats of Russia or France, or of the aristocrats of a Venetian Senate. And I do believe that if the Almighty has not decreed that man shall never be free (and it is blasphemy to believe it), that the secret will be found to be in the making himself the depository of the powers respecting himself, so far as he is competent to them,

and delegating only what is beyond his competence by a synthetical process, to higher and higher orders of functionaries, so as to trust fewer and fewer powers in proportion as the trustees become more and more oligarchical.
  – Thomas Jefferson, Letter to Joseph Cabell, 1816

[T]he States can best govern our home concerns and the general government our foreign ones. I wish, therefore … never to see all offices transferred to Washington, where, further withdrawn from the eyes of the people, they may more secretly be bought and sold at market.
  – Thomas Jefferson, Letter to Judge William Johnson, 1823

THE CONSTITUTION ESTABLISHED A "COMPOUND REPUBLIC" AS A "DOUBLE SECURITY TO THE RIGHTS OF THE PEOPLE" BY WHICH THE STATES AND FEDERAL GOVERNMENT "WILL CONTROL EACH OTHER [FEDERALISM], AT THE SAME TIME THAT EACH WILL BE CONTROLLED BY ITSELF [SEPARATION OF POWERS]."

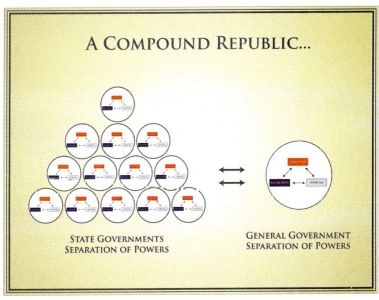

The United States is a Compound Republic Where State and General Governments Must Keep Each Other in Check

James Madison distinguished our compound republic from a single, consolidated republic in these words:

> In a single republic, all the power surrendered by the people is submitted to the administration of a single government; and the usurpations are guarded against by a division of the government into distinct and separate departments. IN THE COMPOUND REPUBLIC OF AMERICA, THE POWER SURRENDERED BY THE PEOPLE IS FIRST DIVIDED BETWEEN TWO DISTINCT GOVERNMENTS, and then the portion allotted to each subdivided among distinct and separate departments.
> – James Madison, Federalist 51, 1788 (emphasis added)

Madison added that the specific reason for establishing a compound republic was to divide constitutional powers between the states and the federal government so the states would check and control unauthorized federal action:

> HENCE A DOUBLE SECURITY ARISES TO THE RIGHTS OF THE PEOPLE. THE DIFFERENT GOVERNMENTS WILL CONTROL EACH OTHER, at the same time that each will be controlled by itself.
> – James Madison, Federalist 51, 1788 (emphasis added)

Alexander Hamilton added the following:

> THIS BALANCE BETWEEN THE NATIONAL AND STATE GOVERNMENTS ought to be dwelt on with peculiar attention, as IT IS OF THE UTMOST IMPORTANCE. IT FORMS A DOUBLE SECURITY TO THE PEOPLE. If one encroaches on their rights they will find a powerful protection in the other. Indeed, THEY WILL BOTH BE PREVENTED FROM OVER PASSING THEIR CONSTITUTIONAL LIMITS BY A CERTAIN RIVALSHIP, which will ever subsist between them.
> – Alexander Hamilton, speech to the New York Ratifying Convention, 1788 (emphasis added)

THE FOUNDERS WERE GUIDED BY CERTAIN FOUNDATIONAL PRINCIPLES, WHICH AS APPLIED TO GOVERNMENT, FUNCTION TO COUNTERBALANCE THE INHERENT TENDENCY OF MAN AND GOVERNMENTS TO AMASS UNBRIDLED POWER:

- Man's unalienable rights come from the Creator (not from a government or a court).

    This "self-evident truth" is recorded in the Declaration of Independence:

    We hold these truths to be self-evident, that all men are created equal, that they ARE ENDOWED BY THEIR CREATOR WITH CERTAIN UNALIENABLE RIGHTS, that among these are Life, Liberty and the pursuit of Happiness.

- Government powers come only from the consent of the governed (not from a government or court).

    In the Declaration of Independence and the Preamble to the Constitution of the United States, respectively, we find the following:

    That to secure these rights, Governments are instituted among Men, *deriving their just powers from the consent of the governed*.

    We The People ... do ordain and establish this Constitution for the United States of America.

THE FOUNDERS DELIBERATELY DESIGNED A UNIQUE CONSTITUTIONAL REPUBLIC ("THE RULE OF LAW, NOT OF MEN") AS THE FORM OF GOVERNMENT BEST SUITED TO PROTECT MAN'S RIGHTS AGAINST TYRANNICAL TENDENCIES.

The Constitution erects the rule of law, not of mere whim or discretion of man, as the basis for our republic.

> The true idea of a republic is 'AN EMPIRE OF LAWS, AND NOT OF MEN.' That, as a republic is the best of governments, so that particular arrangement of the powers of society, or in other words, that form of government which is best contrived to secure an impartial and exact execution of the law, is the best of republics.
> – John Adams, Thoughts on Government, 1776 (emphasis added)

> They define a republic to be a government of laws, and not of men.
> – John Adams, Novanglus No. 7, March 6, 1775 (emphasis added)

> In matters of Power, let no more be heard of confidence in men, but bind him down from mischief by the chains of the Constitution.
> – Thomas Jefferson, Resolutions Relative to the Alien and Sedition Acts, 1798

> The Constitution is not an instrument for the government to restrain the people, it is an instrument for the people to restrain the government — lest it come to dominate our lives and interests.
> – Patrick Henry

THE FOUNDERS DELIBERATELY DESIGNED THE CONSTITUTION EXPRESSLY TO LIMIT POWERS DELEGATED TO THE FEDERAL GOVERNMENT.

James Madison described the constitutional balance of powers between the states and the federal government as follows:

> The powers delegated by the proposed Constitution to the Federal Government, are *FEW AND DEFINED*. Those which are to remain in the State Governments are *NUMEROUS AND INDEFINITE*. The former will be exercised principally on external objects, as war, peace, negotiation, and foreign commerce; with which last the power of taxation will for the most part be connected. The powers reserved to the several States will extend to all the objects, which, in the ordinary course of affairs, concern the lives, liberties and properties of the people; and the internal order, improvement, and prosperity of the State.
> – James Madison, Federalist No. 45, 1788 (emphasis added)

> [T]he powers of the federal government are enumerated; it can only operate in certain cases; it has legislative powers on defined and limited objects, beyond which it cannot extend its jurisdiction.
> – James Madison, Speech at the Virginia Ratifying Convention, June 6, 1788

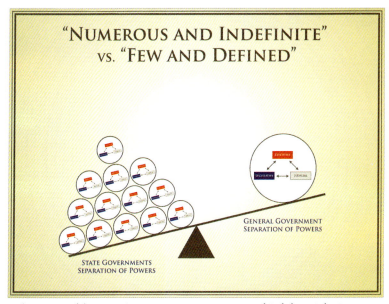

The Powers of the State Government Are Numerous and Indefinite. The Powers of the General Government Are Few and Defined.

THE FRAMERS OF THE CONSTITUTION ESTABLISHED A NETWORK OF CHECKS AND BALANCES TO CURB FEDERAL POWER.

A central problem the Framers addressed was the tendency of government to accumulate unbridled power.

> It may be a reflection on human nature, that such devices should be necessary to control the abuses of government. But what is government itself, but the greatest of all reflections on human nature? If men were angels, no government would be necessary. *IF ANGELS WERE TO GOVERN MEN, NEITHER EXTERNAL NOR INTERNAL CONTROLS ON GOVERNMENT WOULD BE NECESSARY.* In framing a government which is to be administered by men over men, the great difficulty lies in this: you must first enable the government to control the governed; and in the next place oblige it to control itself. A dependence on the people is, no doubt, the primary control on the government; but experience has taught mankind *THE NECESSITY OF AUXILIARY PRECAUTIONS.*
> – James Madison, Federalist 51, 1788 (emphasis added)

It is important, likewise, that THE HABITS OF THINKING IN A FREE COUNTRY SHOULD INSPIRE CAUTION IN THOSE ENTRUSTED WITH ITS ADMINISTRATION, TO CONFINE THEMSELVES WITHIN THEIR RESPECTIVE CONSTITUTIONAL SPHERES; AVOIDING IN THE EXERCISE OF THE POWERS OF ONE DEPARTMENT TO ENCROACH UPON ANOTHER. The spirit of encroachment tends to consolidate the powers of all the departments in one, and thus to create whatever the form of government, a real despotism. A just estimate of that love of power, and proneness to abuse it, which predominates in the human heart is sufficient to satisfy us of the truth of this position. THE NECESSITY OF RECIPROCAL CHECKS IN THE EXERCISE OF POLITICAL POWER, BY DIVIDING AND DISTRIBUTING IT INTO DIFFERENT DEPOSITORIES, AND CONSTITUTING EACH THE GUARDIAN OF THE PUBLIC WEAL ["COMMON GOOD"] AGAINST INVASIONS BY THE OTHERS, has been evinced by experiments ancient and modern; some of them in our country and under our own eyes. TO PRESERVE THEM ["RECIPROCAL CHECKS"] MUST BE AS NECESSARY AS TO INSTITUTE THEM.
– George Washington, Farewell Address, 1796 (emphasis added)

An elective despotism was not the government we fought for, but one which should not only be founded on true free principles, but in which THE POWERS OF GOVERNMENT SHOULD BE SO DIVIDED AND BALANCED AMONG GENERAL BODIES OF MAGISTRACY, AS THAT NO ONE COULD TRANSCEND THEIR LEGAL LIMITS WITHOUT BEING EFFECTUALLY CHECKED AND RESTRAINED BY THE OTHERS.
– Thomas Jefferson, Notes on Virginia, 1792

HAS THE FEDERAL GOVERNMENT LIMITED ITSELF TO ITS "FEW AND DEFINED" POWERS?

Today, the powers assumed and exercised by the federal government are anything but "few and defined." Rather, the federal government has assumed nearly unlimited authority over every aspect of Americans' daily lives. The federal government often exercises this authority through unintelligible one thousand-plus-page bills, which most members of Congress do not bother to read.[2] In the process, the federal government is:

1. Overspending at the rate of more than $1 trillion per year, with plans to overspend at this rate for at least the next ten years (Congressional Budget Office);
2. Amassing a national debt in excess of $14 Trillion (U.S. Treasury);
3. Incurring a net present value of unfunded obligations for Medicare, Medicaid and Social Security in excess of $100 trillion (Dallas Federal Reserve); and
4. Operating through a privately-owned Federal Reserve Bank that is openly creating money out of thin air to fund continued federal overspending and the rollover of maturing debt. Our national fiscal and monetary recklessness is causing great dismay within the world community that had been funding our previous, lower levels of deficit spending.[3]

Perhaps the most enduring example of bipartisanship in Washington D.C. during our lifetime has been the consolidation of power to Washington at the expense of the people, the states, and all future generations of Americans. In short, as Ronald Reagan said, *"the federal government has taken too much tax money from the people, too much authority from the states, and too much liberty with the Constitution."* (Address to Indiana State Legislature, 1982)

> The principle of spending money to be paid by posterity, under the name of funding, is but a swindling futurity on a large scale.
> – Thomas Jefferson, Letter to John Taylor, 1816

> To preserve our independence, we must not let our rulers load us with perpetual debt. We must make our election between economy

---

[2] Examples include the Education-Jobs Bill mandating that states accept federal funds for education, otherwise the federal government will directly appropriate and legislate funds to local education agencies within the states (and singling out Texas by name for adverse treatment); TARP; bailouts of Fannie Mae and Freddie Mac; a stimulus bill passed over a weekend without being read by most members of Congress; national healthcare legislation passed on a rushed vote; the FDA Food Safety Modernization Act; and Build America Bonds whereby prudent states contribute to the debt service costs of financially-challenged states. Outside of Congress, administrative agencies pursue a similar agenda. Recent examples include the EPA attempt to ban lead in bullets and its ongoing efforts to implement a cap-and-trade system by regulation, the FEC decision to institute "net neutrality," and the Interior Secretary claiming unilateral authority to tie up millions of acres of western lands.

[3] "Think what you do when you run in debt; you give to another power over your liberty."
– Benjamin Franklin, The Way to Wealth, 1758

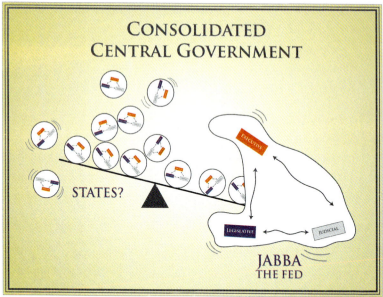

The Federal Government Has Assumed Unlimited Authority over the States and the People

and liberty, or profusion and servitude. I place economy among the first and most important of republican virtues, and public debt as the greatest of the dangers to be feared.
— Thomas Jefferson, Letter to Samuel Kercheval, 1816

It will be of little avail to the people that the laws are made by men of their own choice, if the laws be so voluminous that they cannot be read, or so incoherent that they cannot be understood; if they be repealed or revised before they are promulgated, or undergo such incessant changes that no man who knows what the law is today can guess what it will be tomorrow.
— James Madison, Federalist 62, 1788

Those most involved in the constitutional convention, in the drafting and ratification of the United States Constitution, and the unique system of government engineered thereby, referred with measured reverence to the final work as "a miracle." Just a small sampling of this sentiment follows.

George Washington, who presided over the convention, proclaimed:

> It appears to me, then, LITTLE SHORT OF A MIRACLE, that the Delegates from so many different States ... should unite in forming a system of national Government, so little liable to well founded objections.
> – Letter to Marquis de Lafayette, 1788

James Madison, one of the primary drafters of the Constitution, concurred:

> The happy Union of these States is a wonder; THEIR CONSTITUTION A MIRACLE; their example the hope of Liberty throughout the world.
> – Outline, 1829

Alexander Hamilton, author of fifty-one of the Federalist Papers essays, said of the Constitution:

> For my own part, I sincerely esteem it A SYSTEM, WHICH WITHOUT THE FINGER OF GOD, NEVER COULD HAVE BEEN SUGGESTED AND AGREED UPON by such a diversity of interest.
> – Statement after Constitutional Convention, 1787

Even the great British statesman and four-time Prime Minister, William Gladstone, was compelled to proclaim of our Constitution that it is:

> The most wonderful work ever struck off at a given time by the brain and purpose of man.
> – Life and Public Services, 1899

One of the greatest fundamentals of our "miraculous" constitutional system of government is the division of sovereignty between the states and the national government. Of this, Dallin Oaks, a former justice of the Utah Supreme Court, said:

> This division of sovereignty was unprecedented in theory or practice. In a day when it is fashionable to assume that the [federal] government has the power and means to right every wrong, we should remember that the U.S. Constitution limits the national government to the exercise of powers expressly granted to it. The Tenth Amendment provides:

> The powers not delegated to the United States by the Constitution, nor prohibited to it by the States, are reserved to the States respectively or to the people.
>
> This principle of limited national powers, with all residuary powers reserved to the people or to the state and local governments, which are most responsive to the people, is one of the great fundamentals of the U.S. Constitution.
>
> – Dallin H. Oaks, "The Divinely Inspired Constitution," Ensign, February 1992, 68–74

Can we with impunity disregard, in any degree, this fundamental aspect of our ingenious Constitution "so little liable to well founded objections" without offending the spirit of reverence with which our Founders approached their stewardship over the establishment of our nation?

Can we allow our compound republic—specifically designed so that "the power surrendered by the People is first divided between two distinct governments [states and national government]" in order that they will "control each other" as a "double security to the rights of the people"— to devolve in theory, in education, in expectation, or in practice to any other form or system of government and still expect the blessings of liberty, of peace, and of prosperity for which this constitutional system was "miraculously" devised?

Shall we not commit all the powers at our disposal to study, to teach, and to secure public policies that will preserve and maintain this compound republic system of government for which our forebears were willing to "pledge [their] lives, [their] fortunes, and [their] sacred honor" that we might have liberty, and peace, and prosperity? Because, as Thomas Jefferson famously reminds:

> "If a nation expects to be ignorant and free, ... it expects what never was and never will be."
> – Letter to Col. Charles Yancey, 1816

The Rights, Powers and Duties of State Legislatures

CONSTITUTIONALLY, STATE LEGISLATURES WERE ENTRUSTED WITH RESISTING EVERY FEDERAL USURPATION, BETTER "THAN ANY OTHER POWER ON EARTH CAN DO."

James Madison summarized this principle in these words:

> [T]he State Legislatures will jealously and closely watch the operations of this Government, and BE ABLE TO RESIST WITH MORE EFFECT EVERY ASSUMPTION OF POWER, THAN ANY OTHER POWER ON EARTH CAN DO; and the greatest opponents to a Federal Government admit the State Legislatures to be SURE GUARDIANS OF THE PEOPLE'S LIBERTY.
> – James Madison, Introduction of the Bill of Rights, The Annals of Congress, House of Representatives, First Congress, 1st Session, 448-460, 1789 (emphasis added)

THE STATE LEGISLATORS ARE CONSTITUTIONALLY CHARGED BY SOLEMN OATH WITH "ERECTING SUCH BARRIERS AT THE CONSTITUTIONAL LINE AS CANNOT BE SURMOUNTED EITHER BY THEMSELVES OR BY THE GENERAL GOVERNMENT."

The indispensable responsibility of the states, and of state officers, for the maintenance of our compound republic, as preserved by internal and external checks and balances, is plainly manifest from the direct mandate in Article VI of the Constitution of the United States that

> ... THE MEMBERS OF THE SEVERAL STATE LEGISLATURES, and all executive and judicial Officers, BOTH OF THE UNITED STATES AND OF THE SEVERAL STATES, shall be bound by Oath or Affirmation, to support this Constitution ... (emphasis added)

In the 1966 Academy Award winning movie *A Man for All Seasons*, Sir Thomas More, former Chancellor of England, was being held in the Tower of London (and was subsequently beheaded) for his refusal to swear an oath that was contrary to the dictates of his conscience. His daughter, Meg, was pressured to persuade him to succumb to the oath.

The following dialogue ensued:

> MEG: Father, swear to the Act and come out. ... God more regards the thoughts of the heart than the words of the mouth, or so you've always told me.
>
> MORE: Yes.
>
> MEG: Then say the words of the oath and in your heart think otherwise.
>
> MORE: What is an oath then but words we say to God?
> (Pause)
>
> MORE: Listen Meg, when a man takes an oath he's holding his own self in his own hands like water, and if he opens his fingers then, he needn't hope to find himself again. Some men aren't capable of this. But, I'd be loath to think your father one of them.

Certainly, the Founders, in the economy of words that comprise the Constitution, did not intend for the compulsory oath of office for state officers (or anyone else for that matter) to be merely ceremonial. Rather, the oath was, and is, to be a solemn undertaking of a "sacredly obligatory" duty, as described by George Washington in his Farewell Address:

> ... the Constitution which at any time exists, 'till changed by an explicit and authentic act of the whole People, is SACREDLY OBLIGATORY UPON ALL ...
> – George Washington, 1796 (emphasis added)

And what of the duty for which states and state officers swear a solemn oath to perform? What role are the states to play in supporting and defending the Constitution of the United States?

Thomas Jefferson clearly and unmistakably summarizes the sum and substance of the fundamental duty of the states and state officers in the following words:

> It is important to strengthen the State governments; and as this cannot be done by any change in the Federal Constitution (for the preservation of that is all we need contend for), IT MUST BE DONE BY THE STATES THEMSELVES, ERECTING SUCH BARRIERS AT THE CONSTITUTIONAL LINE AS CANNOT BE SURMOUNTED EITHER BY THEMSELVES OR BY THE GENERAL GOVERNMENT. The only barrier in their power is a wise government. A weak one will lose ground in every contest.
> – Thomas Jefferson, Letter to Archibald Stuart, 1791 (emphasis added)

James Wilson, a signer of the Declaration of Independence and a major force in drafting the Constitution, cited "the accuracy with which the line is drawn between the powers of the federal government and those of the particular state governments" in urging Pennsylvania to ratify the Constitution.

> There is another subject with regard to which this Constitution deserves approbation [praise]. I mean the accuracy with which THE LINE IS DRAWN BETWEEN THE POWERS OF THE GENERAL GOVERNMENT AND THOSE OF THE PARTICULAR STATE GOVERNMENTS ... It is not pretended that the line is drawn with mathematical precision; the inaccuracy of language must, to a certain degree, prevent the accomplishment of such a desire. Whoever views the matter in a true light, will see that THE POWERS ARE AS MINUTELY ENUMERATED AND DEFINED AS WAS POSSIBLE, and will also discover that the general clause, against which so much exception is taken, is nothing more than what was necessary to render effectual the particular powers that are granted.
>
> But let us suppose ... that there is some difficulty in ascertaining WHERE THE TRUE LINE LIES. Are we therefore thrown into despair? Are disputes between the general government and the state governments to be necessarily the consequence of inaccuracy? I hope, sir, they will not be the enemies of each other, or resemble comets in conflicting orbits, mutually operating destruction; BUT THAT THEIR MOTION WILL BE BETTER REPRESENTED BY THAT OF THE PLANETARY SYSTEM, WHERE EACH PART MOVES HARMONIOUSLY WITHIN ITS PROPER SPHERE, and no injury arises by interference or opposition. Every part, I trust, will be considered as a part of the United States. Can any cause of distrust arise here? Is there any increase of risk? Or, rather, ARE NOT THE ENUMERATED POWERS AS WELL DEFINED HERE, AS IN THE PRESENT ARTICLES OF CONFEDERATION?
> – James Wilson, Pennsylvania Ratifying Convention, December 1787 (emphasis added)

Have we lost track of the fundamental constitutional responsibilities whereby the states exert indispensible, external controls over an unruly federal government? Does it not seem today like the federal government "child" is not only setting its own bedtime, but also dictating the curfew of its "parents," the People, and its "older siblings," the states?

Jefferson added:

> I wish to preserve the line drawn by the Federal Constitution between the general and particular governments as it stands at present, and to take every prudent means of preventing either from stepping over it.
> – Thomas Jefferson, 1st Inaugural Address, 1801

This issue of creating a line between two governing powers with respect to the same population, each to be sovereign in their respective spheres, was deemed impossible by Great Britain (and the rest of the known world). In a debate on the subject in 1773 between Thomas Hutchinson, the royal governor of Massachusetts, and John Adams, Hutchinson quipped, *"I know of no line that can be drawn between the supreme authority of Parliament and the total independence of the colonies."*

In response, Adams retorted:

> If there be no such line, the consequence is either that the colonies are vassals of Parliament, or that they are totally independent.
> – John Adams, Letter to Royal Governor Thomas Hutchinson, 1773

More than anything, it was the inability to come to terms on a system of divided sovereignty that led to the total separation and declaration of independence of the Colonies from Great Britain.

As much as anything (if not more so), it was the establishment of this constitutional line, this innovative system of divided sovereignty between the states and the federal government—the genius of this compound republic—that unleashed and secured the laws of liberty, the principles of prosperity, and the pillars of peace to the people of the several states in this new United States of America.

Jefferson added regarding the imperative duty of the states in the operation and maintenance of this distinctive compound republic:

> I am for preserving to the States the powers not yielded by them to the Union, and to the legislature of the Union its constitutional share in the division of powers; and I am not for transferring all the powers of the States to the General Government, and all those of that government to the executive branch.
>
> The support of the State governments in all their rights, as the most competent administrations for our domestic concerns and the surest bulwarks against antirepublican tendencies, I deem [one of] the essential principles of our Government, and consequently [one of] those which ought to shape its administration.
> – Thomas Jefferson, 1st Inaugural Address, 1801

Alexander Hamilton confirms this constitutional charge to the state legislatures in these words:

> WE MAY SAFELY RELY ON THE DISPOSITION OF THE STATE LEGISLATURES to erect barriers against the encroachments of the national authority.
> – Federalist 85, 1788 (emphasis added)

> It may safely be received as an axiom in our political system, that the State governments will, in all possible contingencies, AFFORD COMPLETE SECURITY AGAINST INVASIONS OF THE PUBLIC LIBERTY BY THE NATIONAL AUTHORITY.
> – Federalist 28, 1787 (emphasis added)

Safeguarding the sovereignty of the states is vital to the Union itself.

Samuel Adams (the "Father of the Revolution") affirmed that the sovereignty and jurisdiction of the states is not merely a matter of political jealousy, but is the indispensable linchpin for preserving a republican form of government over such a wide expanse of people and territory:

> I was particularly afraid that unless great care should be taken to prevent it, the Constitution in the Administration of it would gradually, but swiftly and imperceptibly run into a consolidated Government pervading and legislating through all the States, not for federal purposes only as it professes, but in all cases whatsoever: SUCH A GOVERNMENT WOULD SOON TOTALLY ANNIHILATE THE SOVEREIGNTY OF THE SEVERAL STATES SO NECESSARY TO THE SUPPORT OF THE CONFEDERATED COMMONWEALTH, AND SINK BOTH IN DESPOTISM.
> – Samuel Adams, Letter to Richard Henry Lee, 1789 (emphasis added)

Thomas Jefferson added:

- [We have seen] the importance of preserving to the State authorities all that vigor which the Constitution foresaw would be necessary, not only for their own safety, but for that of the whole.
  – Letter to Edward Tiffin, 1807

- I am firmly persuaded that it is by giving due tone to the particular governments that the general one will be preserved in vigor also, the Constitution having foreseen its incompetency to all the objects of government and therefore confined it to those specially described.
  – Letter to James Sullivan, 1791

- [T]he true barriers of our liberty in this country are our state governments.
  – Letter to A.L.C. Destutt de Tracy, 1811

Just as a bicycle is not designed to operate with one bloated tire and one flat one, our compound republic was not designed to function with a bloated federal government and flat state governments.

We have seen lately that it is possible to strain the chain, pressure the pedals, and make the "bicycle of state" continue to move laboriously down the road. But, unless the system is restored to its factory settings and ***both tires*** properly inflated, the strain and pressure will likely endanger safe passage to the liberty, the peace and the prosperity for which it was invented.

A modern U.S. Supreme Court opinion agrees:

> The Constitution does not protect the sovereignty of States for the benefit of the States or state governments as abstract political entities, or even for the benefit of the public officials governing the States. TO THE CONTRARY, THE CONSTITUTION DIVIDES AUTHORITY BETWEEN FEDERAL AND STATE GOVERNMENTS FOR THE PROTECTION OF INDIVIDUALS. STATE SOVEREIGNTY IS NOT JUST AN END IN ITSELF: 'RATHER, FEDERALISM SECURES TO CITIZENS THE LIBERTIES THAT DERIVE FROM THE DIFFUSION OF SOVEREIGN POWER.' 'Just as the separation and independence of the coordinate branches of the Federal Government serve to prevent the accumulation of excessive power in any one branch, A HEALTHY BALANCE OF POWER BETWEEN THE STATES AND THE FEDERAL GOVERNMENT WILL REDUCE THE RISK OF TYRANNY AND ABUSE FROM EITHER FRONT.'
> – New York v. U.S., 505 U.S. 144, 181-82 (1992) (emphasis added)

IF THE STATES ALLOW THE FEDERAL GOVERNMENT TO IGNORE THE CONSTITUTIONAL LINE BY INTERFERING IN THE STATES' JURISDICTIONS, "IT WILL BE [THE STATES'] OWN FAULTS."

John Dickinson warned that the states are empowered and duty-bound to prevent the federal government from interfering in the states' sphere of responsibility:

> In short, the government of each state is, and is to be, sovereign and supreme in all matters that relate to each state only. It is to be subordinate barely in those matters that relate to the whole; AND IT WILL BE THEIR OWN FAULTS, IF THE SEVERAL STATES SUFFER THE FEDERAL SOVEREIGNTY TO INTERFERE IN THE THINGS OF THEIR RESPECTIVE JURISDICTIONS.
> – John Dickinson (Fabius), Letter III, 1788 (emphasis added, all caps emphasis in original)

IT IS A SELF-EVIDENT TRUTH THAT EVERY GOVERNMENT MUST RETAIN THE POWER TO SECURE ITS OWN PRESERVATION.

Hamilton affirmed this principle in these words:

> … EVERY GOVERNMENT OUGHT TO CONTAIN IN ITSELF THE MEANS OF ITS OWN PRESERVATION. Every just reasoner will, at first sight, approve an adherence to this rule in the work of the Convention, and will disapprove every deviation from it …
> – Alexander Hamilton, Federalist 59 (emphasis added)

Madison pointed out that this principle applies to both state and federal governments:

> On the other hand, should an unwarrantable measure of the federal government be unpopular in particular states, which would seldom fail to be the case, or even a warrantable measure be so, which may sometimes be the case, THE MEANS OF OPPOSITION TO IT ARE POWERFUL AND AT HAND. The disquietude of the people, their repugnance and perhaps refusal to co-operate with the officers of the union, the frowns of the executive magistracy [officials] of the state, THE EMBARRASSMENTS [i.e., in modern English, the "obstacles"] CREATED BY LEGISLATIVE DEVICES, WHICH WOULD OFTEN BE ADDED ON SUCH OCCASIONS, WOULD [P]OSE IN ANY STATE DIFFICULTIES NOT TO BE DESPISED; would form in a large state very serious impediments, and where the sentiments of several adjoining states happened to be in union, would present obstructions which the federal government would hardly be willing to encounter.
> – Federalist, No. 46, 1788 (emphasis added)

THE RIGHTS, POWERS AND DUTIES OF STATE LEGISLATURES

THE FOUNDERS VIEWED THE POWER AND RESPONSIBILITY OF THE STATES TO PRESERVE AND MAINTAIN THEIR SOVEREIGNTY AS SIMILAR TO THEIR POWER AND RESPONSIBILITY TO REPEL "THE DREAD OF A FOREIGN YOKE."

Madison urged ratification of the Constitution by assuring the public that under the proposed Constitution states would retain the power and the duty to preserve the balance of power between the states and the federal government:[4]

> *BUT AMBITIOUS ENCROACHMENTS OF THE FEDERAL GOVERNMENT, ON THE AUTHORITY OF THE STATE GOVERNMENTS,* would not excite the opposition of a single state or of a few states only. They would be signals of general alarm. Every government would espouse the common cause. A correspondence would be opened. *PLANS OF RESISTANCE WOULD BE CONCERTED.* One spirit would animate and conduct the whole. The same combinations in short would result from an apprehension of the federal, as was produced by the dread of a foreign yoke; and unless the projected innovations should be voluntarily renounced, the same appeal to a trial of force would be made in the one case, as was made in the other.
> – Federalist 46, 1788 (emphasis added)

---

[4] See also Federalist 28, wherein Hamilton expressed similar views. Yet another Framer, John Dickinson, described the duty of vigilance in this manner: "Another truth respecting the vigilance with which a free people should guard their liberty, that deserves to be carefully observed, is this —that a real tyranny may prevail in a state, while the forms of a free constitution remain."
– John Dickinson, "Notes" in Political Writings (emphasis in original)

THE CONSTITUTIONAL LINE

As emphasized previously, it is the constitutional duty of the states to *"erect such barriers at the constitutional line as cannot be surmounted either by themselves or by the General Government."* Thomas Jefferson defined this "constitutional line" drawn by the Founders in the following unmistakable terms:

> I consider the foundation of the Constitution as laid on this ground: That "all powers not delegated to the United States, by the Constitution, nor prohibited by it to the States, are reserved to the States or to the people" [10th Amendment]. *TO TAKE A SINGLE STEP BEYOND THE BOUNDARIES THUS SPECIFICALLY DRAWN AROUND THE POWERS OF CONGRESS IS TO TAKE POSSESSION OF A BOUNDLESS FIELD OF POWER, NO LONGER SUSCEPTIBLE OF ANY DEFINITION.*
> – Thomas Jefferson: National Bank Opinion, 1791 (emphasis added)

ON ONE SIDE OF THE CONSTITUTIONAL LINE ARE THE POWERS DELEGATED TO THE FEDERAL GOVERNMENT BY THE CONSTITUTION. ON THE OTHER SIDE ARE RESERVED TO THE STATES OR TO THE PEOPLE ALL OTHER POWERS NOT DELEGATED TO THE FEDERAL GOVERNMENT (EXCLUDING ONLY THOSE FEW THAT THE CONSTITUTION SPECIFICALLY PROHIBITS TO THE STATES).

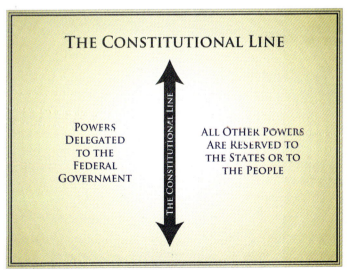

The Constitutional Line Between the Powers of the Federal Government and the States

Throughout the Constitution and the Bill of Rights, enumerations of powers are made to Congress, to the President, and to the Supreme Court. Since 1791, the people have added to the federal government the authority to enforce certain amendments: the Thirteenth (abolition of slavery), Fourteenth (guarding people from certain state abuses), Sixteenth (dropping the rule that income taxes must be apportioned among states), Twentieth (presidential succession), and the Fifteenth, Nineteenth, Twenty-Third, and Twenty-Fourth (extending and protecting the right to vote). The people granted (Eighteenth Amendment) and withdrew (Twenty-First) the power to prohibit alcoholic beverages, and withdrew the power to grant a pay raise to a sitting Congress (Twenty-Seventh).

A list of the specifically enumerated powers delegated to the federal government is set forth in **Appendix A**.

THE "SAFE AND HONEST MEANING" OF OUR WRITTEN CONSTITUTION IS FOUND IN THE PLAIN UNDERSTANDING OF ITS DRAFTERS "AT THE TIME OF ITS ADOPTION."

The Founders firmly rejected the British system of a "living constitution." Instead, they set forth rules in a written document. They gave the document some flexibility through the Article V amendment process, but squarely warned against distorting its original meaning as advocated by proponents of the "living constitution" theory.

> The Constitution on which our Union rests, shall be administered by me [as President] according to the safe and honest meaning contemplated by the plain understanding of the people of the United States at the time of its adoption.
> – Thomas Jefferson, Reply to Address, 1801

> On every question of construction, let us carry ourselves back to the time when the Constitution was adopted, recollect the spirit manifested in the debates, and instead of trying what meaning may be squeezed out of the text, or invented against it, conform to the probable one in which it was passed.
> – Thomas Jefferson, Letter to William Johnson, 1823

> Laws are made for men of ordinary understanding and should, therefore, be construed by the ordinary rules of common sense. Their meaning is not to be sought for in metaphysical subtleties which

may make anything mean everything or nothing at pleasure.
— Thomas Jefferson, Letter to William Johnson, 1823

We must confine ourselves to the powers described in the Constitution, and the moment we pass it, we take an arbitrary stride towards a despotic Government.
— James Jackson, First Congress, 1st Annals of Congress, 1789, 489

This plain and original interpretation of constitutional language prevailed for 150 years. In 1905, for example, the U.S. Supreme Court wrote:

THE CONSTITUTION IS A WRITTEN INSTRUMENT. AS SUCH, ITS MEANING DOES NOT ALTER. THAT WHICH IT MEANT WHEN IT WAS ADOPTED, IT MEANS NOW.
— South Carolina v. United States, 199 U.S. 437, 448 (1905) (emphasis added)

The Founders rejected any "metaphysical" "metamorphosis of the Constitution into a character which ... was not contemplated by its creators" (Madison), whether by means of strained readings of the General Welfare, Necessary and Proper, or Commerce Clauses — or of any other constitutional provision.

If Congress can employ money indefinitely to the general welfare, and are the sole and supreme judges of the general welfare, they may take the care of RELIGION into their own hands; THEY MAY APPOINT TEACHERS IN EVERY STATE, COUNTY AND PARISH AND PAY THEM OUT OF THEIR PUBLIC TREASURY; they may take into their own hands THE EDUCATION OF CHILDREN, ESTABLISHING IN LIKE MANNER SCHOOLS THROUGHOUT THE UNION; THEY MAY ASSUME THE PROVISION OF THE POOR; they may undertake THE REGULATION OF ALL ROADS OTHER THAN POST-ROADS; in short, EVERY THING, FROM THE HIGHEST OBJECT OF STATE LEGISLATION DOWN TO THE MOST MINUTE OBJECT OF POLICE, would be thrown under the power of Congress ... WERE THE POWER OF CONGRESS TO BE ESTABLISHED IN THE LATITUDE CONTENDED FOR, IT WOULD SUBVERT THE VERY FOUNDATIONS, AND TRANSMUTE THE VERY NATURE OF THE LIMITED GOVERNMENT ESTABLISHED BY THE PEOPLE OF AMERICA."
— James Madison, First U.S. Congress Floor Debate, 1792 (emphasis added)

With respect to the words "general welfare," I have always regarded them as qualified by the detail of powers connected with them. To take them in a literal and unlimited sense would be a metamorphosis of the Constitution into a character which THERE IS A HOST OF PROOFS WAS NOT CONTEMPLATED BY ITS CREATORS.
– James Madison, Letter to James Robertson, 1831 (emphasis added)

I cannot undertake to lay my finger upon an article of the Constitution which granted a right to Congress of expending, on the objects of benevolence, the money of their constituents.
– James Madison, Annals of Congress, 3rd Congress, 170, 1794

Congress has not unlimited powers to provide for the general welfare, but only those specifically enumerated.
– Thomas Jefferson, Letter to Albert Gallatin, 1817

[The federal government] cannot interfere with the opening of rivers and canals; the making or regulation of roads, except post roads; building bridges; erecting ferries; establishment of state seminaries of learning; libraries; literary, religious, trading or manufacturing societies; erecting or regulating the police of cities, towns or boroughs; creating new state offices; building light houses, public wharves, county gaols [jails], markets, or other public buildings; making sale of state lands, and other state property; receiving or appropriating the incomes of state buildings and property; executing the state laws; altering the criminal law; NOR CAN THEY DO ANY OTHER MATTER OR THING APPERTAINING TO THE INTERNAL AFFAIRS OF ANY STATE, WHETHER LEGISLATIVE, EXECUTIVE OR JUDICIAL, CIVIL OR ECCLESIASTICAL.
– Tench Coxe, Freeman No. 1, 1788 (Tench Coxe was a delegate for Pennsylvania to the Continental Congress in 1788-1789) (emphasis added)

This is just one of several such lists published during the ratification debates of areas widely acknowledged at the time as being outside federal control.

By virtue of a written Constitution, the People need not rise up in rebellion at every unauthorized act of government for fear of surrendering their rights by acquiescence to unconstitutional acts of government.

> [The purpose of a written constitution is] to bind up the several branches of government by certain laws, which, when they transgress, their acts shall become nullities; to render unnecessary an appeal to the people, or in other words a rebellion, on every infraction of their rights, on the peril that their acquiescence shall be construed into an intention to surrender those rights.
> – Thomas Jefferson, Notes on Virginia, 1782

THE PLAIN, ORIGINAL MEANING OF THE CONSTITUTION IS "SACREDLY OBLIGATORY UPON ALL" UNLESS AND UNTIL DULY CHANGED BY AN AMENDMENT OF THE PEOPLE.

In light of the careful manner in which the Framers deliberated over each word and phrase of the Constitution, it defies (i) logic, (ii) the very purpose underlying the Constitution, and (iii) the basic rules of constitutional construction, that the Framers intended anything approaching the one sentence "constitution" the federal government is now purporting to impose on us all:

> *The Federal Government shall have supreme power to spend (even money it does not have), in any way which it claims may promote the general welfare, and to regulate or mandate any activity, or even inactivity, which it contends may substantially affect interstate commerce.*

Jefferson said clearly that it was never the intention of the Founders to reduce the Constitution to a "single phrase" granting power to the federal government to do "whatever evil they please."

> It would reduce the whole instrument to a single phrase, that of instituting a Congress with power to do whatever would be for the good of the United States; and as they would be the sole judges of the good or evil, it would be also a power to do whatever evil they please. CERTAINLY NO SUCH UNIVERSAL POWER WAS MEANT TO BE GIVEN THEM. IT [THE CONSTITUTION] WAS INTENDED TO LACE THEM UP STRAIGHTLY WITHIN THE ENUMERATED POWERS and those without which, as means, these powers could not be carried into effect.
> – Thomas Jefferson, Opinion on a National Bank, February 15, 1791 (emphasis added)

> Our peculiar security is in the possession of a written Constitution. Let us not make it a blank paper by construction.
> – Thomas Jefferson, Letter to Wilson Nicholas, 1803

President Washington described the plain language of the Constitution as "sacredly obligatory upon all" "till changed by an explicit act of the whole People." He warned that changes "by usurpation," even, and especially, for "good things" beyond the authority of the federal government, "is the customary weapon by which free governments are destroyed."

> The basis of our political systems is the right of the people to make and to alter their Constitutions of Government. BUT THE CONSTITUTION WHICH AT ANY TIME EXISTS, TILL CHANGED BY AN EXPLICIT AND AUTHENTIC ACT OF THE WHOLE PEOPLE, IS SACREDLY OBLIGATORY UPON ALL ...
>
> If in the opinion of the People, the distribution or modification of the Constitutional powers be in any particular wrong, let it be corrected by an amendment in the way which the Constitution designates. BUT LET THERE BE NO CHANGE BY USURPATION; FOR THOUGH THIS, IN ONE INSTANCE, MAY BE THE INSTRUMENT OF GOOD, IT IS THE CUSTOMARY WEAPON BY WHICH FREE GOVERNMENTS ARE DESTROYED. The precedent must always greatly overbalance in permanent evil any partial or transient benefit which the use can at any time yield.
> – George Washington Farewell Address, 1796 (emphasis added)

As noted above, certain "self-evident truths" are indispensable to the foundation of our constitutional republic: (i) that it is the very nature of men and governments to amass unbridled power; (ii) that unalienable rights come from our Creator, and (iii) that powers delegated to government come from the people ("the governed"). Given these fundamental principles, it is also self-evident that a federal court is without power or authority to create or un-create unalienable rights of man. Similarly, a federal court is without power or authority to delegate or un-delegate powers to itself or its co-extensive federal branches of government.

The "few and defined" powers delegated to the federal government are set forth in the plain language of the Constitution as construed pursuant to the original meaning of those who created it. Fortunately, the Founders left for us a plentiful trail of breadcrumbs to follow their original meaning in their contemporaneous, abundant writings.

AT THE TIME OF THE RATIFICATION OF THE BILL OF RIGHTS IN 1791, THE POWERS "PROHIBITED TO THE STATES" BY THE CONSTITUTION WERE UNDERSTOOD AS THOSE LISTED IN **APPENDIX B**.

AT THE TIME OF THE RATIFICATION OF THE BILL OF RIGHTS IN 1791, THE POWERS "RESERVED TO THE STATES RESPECTIVELY, OR TO THE PEOPLE" WERE CLEARLY UNDERSTOOD AS **ALL OTHER POWERS**, INCLUDING SPECIFICALLY, AND WITHOUT LIMITATION, THOSE LISTED IN **APPENDIX C**.

In addition to describing federal powers as "few and defined," and state powers as "numerous and indefinte," Madison described the balance between states and the federal government as follows:

> *THE STATE GOVERNMENT WILL HAVE THE ADVANTAGE OF THE FEDERAL GOVERNMENT*, whether we compare them in respect to the immediate dependence of the one on the other; to the weight of personal influence which each side will possess; *TO THE POWERS RESPECTIVELY VESTED IN THEM; TO THE PREDILECTION AND PROBABLE SUPPORT OF THE PEOPLE; TO THE DISPOSITION AND FACULTY OF RESISTING AND FRUSTRATING THE MEASURES OF EACH OTHER.*
> – James Madison, Federalist 45, 1788 (emphasis added)

Thomas Jefferson added this:

> When we consider that this Government is charged with the external and mutual relations only of these States; that the States themselves have principal care of our persons, our property, and our reputation, constituting the great field of human concerns, we may well doubt whether our organization is not too complicated, too expensive, whether offices and officers have not been multiplied unnecessarily and sometimes injuriously to the service they were meant to promote.
> – Thomas Jefferson, First Annual Message to Congress, 1801 (emphasis added)

PRIOR FEDERAL GOVERNMENT EFFORTS TO LIMIT ITSELF TO THE FEW POWERS DELEGATED TO IT HAVE FAILED FOR LACK OF THE CONSTITUTIONALLY CRITICAL "EXTERNAL CONTROLS" BY THE STATES.

In 1987, President Ronald Reagan issued Executive Order 12612 titled, "Federalism" (copy attached hereto as **Appendix D**). This was designed to support and defend the principles of federalism (the constitutional distribution of sovereignty, jurisdiction, and power between the national government and the states). However, the legislative and judicial branches did not follow the lead of the President, and his order was revoked in 1998 by President Bill Clinton's superseding Executive Order 13083.

This is a prime example of how action internal to the federal government—such as merely electing good candidates to Congress and the Presidency—is not enough. It is why the Founders inserted *"internal controls"* and *"external controls"* necessary for *"reciprocal checks in the exercise of political power; by dividing and distributing it into different depositories, and constituting each the Guardian of the Public Weal against invasions by the others."* (George Washington, Farewell Address, 1796, emphasis added)

As noted earlier, President Washington endorsed the warning of Framer John Dickinson that *"it will be their own FAULTS, if the several States suffer the federal sovereignty to interfere in the things of their respective jurisdictions."* Thus, the states, as the *"sure guardians of the people's liberty,"* are duty-bound to exercise *"external controls"* over the federal government when it disregards constitutional limits.

> It is important to strengthen the State governments; and as this cannot be done by any change in the Federal Constitution (for the preservation of that is all we need contend for), IT MUST BE DONE BY THE STATES THEMSELVES, ERECTING SUCH BARRIERS AT THE CONSTITUTIONAL LINE AS CANNOT BE SURMOUNTED either by themselves or by the General Government. The only barrier in their power is a wise government. A weak one will lose ground in every contest.
> — Thomas Jefferson, Letter to Archibald Stuart, 1791 (emphasis added)

> [T]HE STATE LEGISLATURES WILL JEALOUSLY AND CLOSELY WATCH THE OPERATIONS OF THIS GOVERNMENT, AND BE ABLE TO RESIST WITH MORE EFFECT EVERY ASSUMPTION OF POWER, THAN ANY OTHER POWER ON EARTH CAN DO; and the greatest opponents to a Federal Government admit the State Legislatures to be SURE GUARDIANS OF THE PEOPLE'S LIBERTY.
> — James Madison, Introduction of the Bill of Rights, The Annals of Congress, House of Representatives, First Congress, 1st Session, 448-460, 1789 (emphasis added)

THE CONSTITUTIONAL LINE

So often today, state lawmakers marshal scarce resources and spend precious political capital to craft unique solutions to constituents' problems—only to have the federal government shatter those solutions with intrusive, costly, and one-size-fits-all edicts. State lawmakers find themselves building elaborate sand castles on a beach where the federal tide perpetually rolls in.

The system is the solution; the system of external controls at the disposal of our state legislatures, which was bequeathed to us by our Founders. Restoring and maintaining the balance of this system requires effort, but how can Americans expect to "secure the blessings of liberty" without price?

> Those who expect to reap the benefits of freedom, must, like men, undergo the fatigue of supporting it.
> — Thomas Paine, The Crisis, 1777

The critical question remains for state legislatures, state legislators, and their respective constituents:

"Where's the Line, America?"

THEREFORE, WHAT ... ?

It is reported that the great coach, Vince Lombardi, started each new season the same way with his world champion, professional football team, the Green Bay Packers: "Gentlemen, this is a football." He would explain the size and shape of the ball and how it was used to win the game. He would then walk his professional players out of the locker room and into the stadium and explain "Gentlemen, this is a football field," and explain the dimensions, where the out of bounds and the end zones are and what role they play in the game, etc.

Utah took a page from the Vince Lombardi playbook during the 2011 legislative session by passing HB76 – The Federal Law Evaluation and Response Act (FLERA), sponsored by the author. In Lombardi-like fashion, this legislation draws upon James Madison and others to coach state government officials in the constitutional fundamentals: "Gentlemen [and Ladies], this is a *Compound Republic*. *'The power surrendered by the People is first divided among two distinct governments'* (federal and the states) and they *'will control each other,'* so that *'a double security arises to the rights of the people.'"*

The Federal Law Evaluation and Response Act (FLERA) is codified at UCA 63C-4-101 et seq. FLERA establishes a systematic and proactive mechanism whereby Utah, in concert with its congressional delegation and with other states, monitors the "constitutional line" and challenges, through a dispute resolution framework, all federal laws, agency actions, or executive orders that cross the line. An outline of this legislation is included in **Appendix E**. You can also read the bill in its entirety at *www.WheresTheLineAmerica.com*.

There is a palpable, and largely non-partisan, sense of the nationwide angst about a federal government devoid of budgetary balance and governmental proportionality. This national discontent cries out for the states to take a concerted and definitive stand in carrying out the fundamental, constitutional duties of the states to:

- Be the *"sure guardians of the people's liberty."* (Madison)
- Prevent the federal government *"from over passing their constitutional limits."* (Hamilton)
- *"Erect barriers at the constitutional line as cannot be surmounted either by themselves or by the General Government."* (Jefferson)
- *"Jealously and closely watch the [federal] government, and be able to resist ...*

WHERE'S THE LINE? 33

every assumption of power, [better] than any other power on earth can do." (Madison)
- And, as Framer John Dickinson said, *"it will be their own FAULTS, if the several states suffer the federal sovereignty to interfere in the things of their respective jurisdictions."* (capital emphasis original)

THE HISTORIC PRECEDENT FOR STATE LEGISLATIVE ACTION LIKE FLERA

Despite the Boston Massacre in 1770, it was not until 1776 that the Colonies declared independence from Great Britain. When Thomas Jefferson, Benjamin Franklin and John Adams were ultimately assigned to draft a declaration of independence, the Continental Congress and its members had already "built the record" over the course of at least six years of the "long train of abuses." So, this drafting committee did not need to research the abuses because the record was already available to all.

There was power in the process of the Colonies' collectively reviewing, evaluating, responding to, and publicly documenting the tyrannical actions of the king and of Parliament. Through this process, the colonists, the Colonies and the members of their Continental Congress, individually and collectively comprehended the full magnitude of their predicament and gained the resolve to pledge their lives, their fortunes, and their sacred honor in the exercise of their rights and their duties to secure, protect, and defend their unalienable, God-given rights.

The comparison in our case is particularly apt, not to the end of declaring independence, but through the exercise of good faith in building a public record, in diagnosing the full magnitude of the predicament, gaining the resolve to exercise all the rights, the powers, and the duties constitutionally charged upon the states to stand firm as the *"sure guardians of the People's liberty"* (Madison), and in preventing the federal government from "over passing their constitutional limits" (Hamilton).

Having experienced the full measure of this process, Alexander Hamilton and James Madison left this counsel to the states for the exercise of their rights and duties in our compound republic:

"It may safely be received as an axiom in our political system, that the State governments will, in all possible contingencies, afford complete security against invasions of the public liberty by the national authority. Projects of usurpation cannot be masked ... The legislatures will have (i) BETTER MEANS OF INFORMATION. They can (ii) DISCOVER THE DANGER at a distance; and (iii) POSSESSING ALL THE ORGANS OF CIVIL POWER, and (iv) the confidence of the people, they can at once (v) ADOPT A REGULAR PLAN OF OPPOSITION, in which they can (vi) COMBINE ALL THE RESOURCES OF THE COMMUNITY. They can (vii) READILY COMMUNICATE WITH EACH OTHER IN THE DIFFERENT STATES, and (viii) UNITE THEIR COMMON FORCES FOR THE PROTECTION OF THEIR COMMON LIBERTY."
– Hamilton, Federalist, No. 28, 1787 (emphasis and numbering added)

But ambitious encroachments of the federal government, on the authority of the State governments, (i) WOULD NOT EXCITE THE OPPOSITION OF A SINGLE STATE, OR OF A FEW STATES ONLY. They would be (ii) SIGNALS OF GENERAL ALARM. Every government would (iii) ESPOUSE THE COMMON CAUSE. A (iv) CORRESPONDENCE WOULD BE OPENED. (v) PLANS OF RESISTANCE WOULD BE CONCERTED. (vi) ONE SPIRIT WOULD ANIMATE AND CONDUCT THE WHOLE. The same combinations, in short, would result from an apprehension of the federal, as was produced by the dread of a foreign, yoke; and unless the projected innovations should be voluntarily renounced, the same appeal to a trial of force would be made in the one case as was made in the other. ... But what would be the contest in the case we are supposing? Who would be the parties? A few representatives of the people would be opposed to the people themselves; or rather (vii) ONE SET OF REPRESENTATIVES WOULD BE CONTENDING AGAINST THIRTEEN SETS OF REPRESENTATIVES, with the (viii) WHOLE BODY OF THEIR COMMON CONSTITUENTS ON THE SIDE OF THE LATTER.
– Madison, Federalist No. 46 (emphasis and numbering added)

After warning the states that "it will be their own FAULTS" if they allowed the federal government to intrude in their jurisdictions, John Dickinson admonished all states to act in concert to secure and preserve their respective and collective jurisdictions as follows:

An instance of such interference with regard to any single state, will be a dangerous precedent as to all, and therefore will be guarded against by all, AS THE TRUSTEES OR SERVANTS OF THE SEVERAL

> STATES WILL NOT DARE, IF THEY RETAIN THEIR SENSES, SO TO VIOLATE THE INDEPENDENT SOVEREIGNTY OF THEIR RESPECTIVE STATES, the justly darling object of American affections, to which they are responsible."
> – Fabius Letter III, 1788

Governors Affirm that Determining the Proper Role of State and Federal Governments "Is neither a Partisan Issue, nor Is It an Issue Dividing Liberals and Conservatives"

Governors generally understand that the states are, and are to be, sovereign entities within their constitutional sphere of responsibilities. Governors generally understand that states are not colonies or mere vassals to a supreme federal power. Rather, they are dual sovereigns in their respective orbits, in an unprecedented system of federalism; a compound republic where "the different governments will control each other." Governors generally understand that under Article VI of the U.S. Constitution, state officials bear a constitutional duty to scrupulously preserve and fight for this system whenever it seems in danger.

> FEDERALISM IS NEITHER A PARTISAN ISSUE, NOR IS IT AN ISSUE DIVIDING LIBERALS AND CONSERVATIVES. It's a philosophical concept of how the federal governmental system operates, AN EFFORT TO DETERMINE THE PROPER ROLE OF STATE AND FEDERAL GOVERNMENTS. Madison particularly saw an ongoing, important role for the states in the federal system and argued, in Federalist number fourteen, that if states were abolished, "the general government would be compelled by the principle of self preservation, to reinstate them in their proper jurisdiction."
> – Gov. Scott Matheson (D-Utah, 1977-1985), Out of Balance, page 18 (emphasis added)

> As a matter of fact and law, THE GOVERNING RIGHTS OF THE STATES ARE ALL OF THOSE WHICH HAVE NOT BEEN SURRENDERED TO THE NATIONAL GOVERNMENT BY THE CONSTITUTION OR ITS AMENDMENTS.
> … Congress has been given the right to legislate on … particular subject[s], but this is not the case in the matter of a great number of other vital problems of government, such as THE CONDUCT OF PUBLIC UTILITIES, OF BANKS, OF INSURANCE, OF BUSINESS, OF AGRICULTURE, OF EDUCATION, OF SOCIAL WELFARE AND

OF A DOZEN OTHER IMPORTANT FEATURES. IN THESE, WASHINGTON MUST NOT BE ENCOURAGED TO INTERFERE ...

NOW, TO BRING ABOUT GOVERNMENT BY OLIGARCHY MASQUERADING AS DEMOCRACY, IT IS FUNDAMENTALLY ESSENTIAL THAT PRACTICALLY ALL AUTHORITY AND CONTROL BE CENTRALIZED IN OUR NATIONAL GOVERNMENT. THE INDIVIDUAL SOVEREIGNTY OF OUR STATES MUST FIRST BE DESTROYED, EXCEPT IN MERE MINOR MATTERS OF LEGISLATION. WE ARE SAFE FROM THE DANGER OF ANY SUCH DEPARTURE FROM THE PRINCIPLES ON WHICH THIS COUNTRY WAS FOUNDED JUST SO LONG AS THE INDIVIDUAL HOME RULE OF THE STATES IS SCRUPULOUSLY PRESERVED AND FOUGHT FOR WHENEVER IT SEEMS IN DANGER.
– Gov. Franklin D. Roosevelt (D-NY, 1928-1932), On States' Rights and Constitutional Authority, March 2, 1930 (emphasis added)

A PRESSING NEED FOR THE RESOLVE TO MAINTAIN THE RIGHTS INHERITED FROM OUR FATHERS FOR THE SAKE OF OUR CHILDREN

The biggest issues that face us today are not fundamentally left or right, liberal or conservative; *they are jurisdictional* and *systemic*. It's *"Where to Decide"* before tackling *"What to Decide;"* it's the unique genius of our constitutional system of divided sovereignty—our compound republic—where *"the two governments (states and federal) will control each other"* and prevent each other from *"over passing their constitutional limits."*

It will not matter "what" the decision is, or which party in control makes the determination, if we allow the federal government to determine things like:
(i) whether or not a special education teacher can continue a bake sale program with her special education students;
(ii) whether all Americans must buy a certain type of health insurance;
(iii) whether states can manage their own lands, and mineral and energy resources, in their state (or whether the federal government will control 70% or more of a state's lands);
(iv) what kind of light bulbs Americans can or cannot use;
(v) how much water all toilets in America can flush;
(vi) what Americans can and cannot sell at home garage sales;
(vii) whether or not Americans can sell privately grown food at a farmer's market or even give it to their neighbor;

(viii) how to teach and test all children at their local school, regardless of their particular local circumstances;
(ix) the regulation of everything about private property in the middle of a desert by claiming a 12-inch wide rivulet amounts to "navigable waters;" or
(x) how much of this generation's debt, interest and entitlements the rising (and all future) generations will have to pay for the rest of their lives because Washington is pathologically addicted to spending "other people's money," etc., etc., etc.

Invariably, such centralized decisions will be too costly, too burdensome, too inflexible, and too infused with motives to perpetuate centralized Washington power and control, and *"will annihilate the sovereignty of the several states so necessary to the support of the confederated commonwealth"!* (Samuel Adams, Letter to Richard Henry Lee, 1789)

Once we constitutionally secure the appropriate *jurisdiction* of a matter (i.e., "Where to Decide"), then we should have great debates over the merits of a particular issue at the appropriate level of government. Safeguarding the appropriate jurisdiction requires the vigilance of the states to maintain our compound republic system where states *"erect barriers at the constitutional line"* so as not to fall into a consolidated government where all substantive government power and attention is drawn to Washington.

Thomas Jefferson repeatedly warned of the dangers of allowing powers beyond those expressly delegated to the national government under the Constitution to be consolidated into one unwieldy government:

- When all government, domestic and foreign, in little as in great things, shall be drawn to Washington as the centre of all power, IT WILL RENDER POWERLESS THE CHECKS PROVIDED OF ONE GOVERNMENT ON ANOTHER, and will become as venal and oppressive as the government from which we separated.
  – Letter to Charles Hammond, 1821

- Our government is now taking so steady a course as to show by what road it will pass to destruction, to wit: by consolidation first, and then corruption, its necessary consequence. The engine of consolidation will be the Federal judiciary; the two other branches the corrupting and corrupted instruments.
  – Letter to Nathaniel Macon, 1821

- To take from the States all the powers of self-government and transfer them to a general and consolidated government, without regard to the special delegations and reservations solemnly agreed to in [the Federal] compact, is not for the peace, happiness or prosperity of these States.
  – Draft Kentucky Resolutions, 1798

- Our country is too large to have all its affairs directed by a single government. Public servants at such a distance, and from under the eye of their constituents, must, from the circumstance of distance, be unable to administer and overlook all the details necessary for the good government of the citizens; and the same circumstance, by rendering detection impossible to their constituents, will invite the public agents to corruption, plunder and waste.
  – Letter to Gideon Granger, 1800

And so, in standing as sentinels at the "constitutional line" so that the people "may safely rely on the disposition of [their] state legislatures to erect barriers against the encroachments of the national authority" (Hamilton), let us with great care and great resolve hear and heed the charge of one of the most ardent Sons of Liberty, Samuel Adams:

> THE LIBERTIES OF OUR COUNTRY, THE FREEDOM OF OUR CIVIL CONSTITUTION ARE WORTH DEFENDING AT ALL HAZARDS: AND IT IS OUR DUTY TO DEFEND THEM AGAINST ALL ATTACKS. We have receiv'd them as a fair Inheritance from our worthy Ancestors: They purchas'd them for us with toil and danger and expence of treasure and blood; and transmitted them to us with care and diligence. It will bring an everlasting mark of infamy on the present generation, enlightened as it is, if we should suffer them to be wrested from us by violence without a struggle; or be cheated out of them by the artifices of false and designing men. Of the latter we are in most danger at present: Let us therefore be aware of it. Let us contemplate our forefathers and posterity; and resolve to maintain the rights bequeath'd to us from the former, for the sake of the latter. -- Instead of sitting down satisfied with the efforts we have already made, which is the wish of our enemies, THE NECESSITY OF THE TIMES, MORE THAN EVER, CALLS FOR OUR UTMOST CIRCUMSPECTION, DELIBERATION, FORTITUDE AND PERSEVERANCE. LET US REMEMBER, THAT "IF WE SUFFER TAMELY A LAWLESS ATTACK UPON OUR LIBERTY, WE ENCOURAGE IT, AND INVOLVE OTHERS IN OUR DOOM." IT IS A VERY SERIOUS CONSIDERATION, WHICH SHOULD DEEPLY IMPRESS OUR MINDS, THAT MILLIONS YET UNBORN

Therefore What ... ?

MAY BE THE MISERABLE SHARERS IN THE EVENT.
– Boston Gazette, 1771 (emphasis added)

As state legislators, we are duty-bound under Article VI of the US Constitution to know, maintain, and defend the "constitutional line." State legislators and officers receive their marching orders and take courage from informed, involved and courageous citizens. It is my desire that each one of us will do all in our power and encourage all within our influence to promote and foster a national dialogue regarding "Where's the Line, America?" Here are some simple ways to focus on doing this:

- **STUDY** – to gain a working understanding of "The Line" as intended between the roles of states and the federal government, where it is now, and measures to restore it.
- **SHARE** – *Where's the Line, America?* with neighbors, friends and family.
- **ASK** – government representatives at every level, *Where's the Line, America?*
- **COMMIT** – time, talents, resources and relationships to building the national, non-partisan dialogue about *Where's the Line, America?*

Learn more about how to add your efforts to foster the growing national dialogue about **Where's the Line, America?** at:

www.WheresTheLineAmerica.com
facebook.com/WheresTheLineAmerica

APPENDICES

APPENDIX A: A TABULATION OF THE "FEW AND DEFINED" POWERS DELEGATED TO CONGRESS AS OF 1791

The Constitution granted powers to each of the three branches of the federal government —Congress, the President, and the Judiciary. Although the principal enumeration was the list of congressional powers in Article I, Section 8, others were placed throughout the document.

Powers of Congress:

- Article I, Section 2, to provide for the decennial census;
- Article I, Section 4, to override state laws regulating the times, places, and manner of congressional elections, other than the place of senatorial elections;
- Article I, Section 8, to:
  - lay and collect taxes, duties, imposts, and excises, to pay the debts and provide for the common defense and general welfare of the United States, but all duties, imposts, and excises shall be uniform throughout the United States (clause 1);
  - borrow money on the credit of the United States (clause 2);
  - regulate commerce with foreign nations, among the several states, and with the Indian tribes (clause 3);
  - establish a uniform rule of naturalization and uniform laws on the subject of bankruptcies throughout the United States (clause 4);
  - coin money, regulate the value of coin money and of foreign coin, and fix the standard of weights and measures (clause 5);
  - provide for the punishment of counterfeiting the securities and current coin of the United States (clause 6);
  - establish post offices and post roads (clause 7);
  - promote the progress of science and useful arts, by securing for limited times to authors and inventors the exclusive right to their respective writings and discoveries (clause 8);
  - constitute tribunals inferior to the supreme court (clause 9);
  - define and punish piracies and felonies committed on the high seas and offences against the law of nations (clause 10);
  - declare war, grant letters of marque and reprisal, and make rules concerning

- captures on land and water (clause 11);
- raise and support armies, but no appropriation of money to that use shall be for a longer term than two years (clause 12);
- provide and maintain a navy (clause 13);
- make rules for the government and regulation of the land and naval forces (clause 14);
- provide for calling forth the militia to execute the laws of the union, suppress insurrections, and repel invasions (clause 15);
- provide for organizing, arming, and disciplining the militia, and for governing the part of the militia that may be employed in the service of the United States, reserving to the states respectively, the appointment of the officers and the authority of training the militia according to the discipline prescribed by Congress (clause 16);
- exercise exclusive legislation in all cases whatsoever, over such district, which may not exceed 10 miles square, as may, by cession of particular states and the acceptance of Congress, become the seat of the government of the United States, and to exercise like authority over all places purchased by the consent of the legislature of the state in which the place shall be, for the erection of forts, magazines, arsenals, dock-yards, and other needful buildings (clause 17); and
- make all laws which shall be necessary and proper for carrying into execution the powers listed in this section, and all other powers vested by the United States Constitution in the government of the United States, or in any department or officer of the United States (clause 18);

- Article I, Section 9, to authorize a federal officer to receive benefits from a foreign nation;
- Article I, Section 10, to fix the pay of members of Congress and of federal officers;
- Article II, Section 1, to:
  - set the time for choosing electors; and
  - establish who succeeded to the presidency after the vice president;
- Article III, Section 1, to:
  - create exceptions to the supreme court's appellate jurisdiction;
  - fix the jurisdiction of federal courts inferior to the supreme court; and
  - declare the punishment for treason;
- Article IV, Section 1, to establish the rules by which the records and judgments of states are proved in other states;

- Article IV, Section 3, to:
  - manage federal property;
  - dispose of federal property;
  - govern the federal territories; and
  - consent to admission of new states or the combination of existing states;
- Article IV, Section 4, to defend states from invasion, insurrection, and non-republican forms of government;
- Article V, Section 1, to propose constitutional amendments;
- Article VI, Section 1, to prescribe the oath for federal officers;

Additional powers delegated by amendments:

- Amendment XIII, to abolish slavery;
- Amendment XIV, to guard people from certain state abuses;
- Amendment XVI, to impose taxes on income from any source without having to apportion the total dollar amount of tax collected from each state according to each state's population in relation to the total national population;
- Amendment XX, to revise the manner of presidential succession;
- Amendment XV, XIX, XXIII, or XXIV, to extend and protect the right to vote; and
- Amendment XVII, to grant a pay raise to a sitting Congress.

Powers of the President:

- Article I, Section 7, to veto bills, orders, and resolutions by Congress;
- Article II, Section 2, to:
  - serve as Commander-in-Chief of the armed forces;
  - require the written opinions of executive officers;
  - grant reprieves and pardons;
  - make vacancy appointments;
  - make treaties, subject to the advice and consent of the United States Senate;
  - appoint foreign affairs officers subject to the advice and consent of the United States Senate;
  - appoint domestic affairs officers subject either to the advice and consent of the United States Senate or pursuant to law;

- appoint judges subject to the advice and consent of the United States Senate; and
- authorize the president to fill designated inferior offices without senatorial consent;
• Article II, Section 3, to:
  - receive representatives of foreign powers;
  - execute the laws;
  - commission United States officers;
  - give Congress information;
  - make recommendations to Congress;
  - convene Congress on extraordinary occasions; and
  - adjourn Congress if it cannot agree on a time;

The Supreme Court was granted:

• Original trial jurisdiction of:
  - Cases affecting representatives of foreign countries;
  - Cases to which a state was a party, subject to the rule (reflected in the Eleventh Amendment) that a state could not be sued by an individual without its consent (Art. III, Sec. 2, cl. 2).
• Appellate jurisdiction was granted over six other kinds of cases, subject to removal by Congress (Art. III, Sec. 2, cls. 1 & 2).
• Lower courts were to be created by Congress, with Congress permitted to assign jurisdiction within limited areas (Art. I, Sec. 8, cl. 9; Art. III, Sec. 1 & Sec. 2, cl. 2).

Appendix B: The Constitutional Line—The Powers Prohibited to the States

1. No State shall:
   a. Enter into any Treaty, Alliance, or Confederation;
   b. Grant Letters of Marque and Reprisal;
   c. Coin Money; emit Bills of Credit;
   d. Make any Thing but gold and silver Coin a Tender in Payment of Debts;
   e. Pass any Bill of Attainder, ex post facto Law, or Law impairing the Obligation of Contracts; or
   f. Grant any Title of Nobility (Art. I, Sec 10, cl. 1).
2. No State shall, without the Consent of the Congress, lay any Imposts or Duties on Imports or Exports, except what may be absolutely necessary for executing its inspection Laws: and the net Produce of all Duties and Imposts, laid by any State on Imports or Exports, shall be for the Use of the Treasury of the United States; and all such Laws shall be subject to the Revision and Control of the Congress (Art. I, Sec 10, cl. 2).
3. No State shall, without the Consent of Congress:
   a. Lay any duty of Tonnage;
   b. Keep Troops, or Ships of War in time of Peace;
   c. Enter into any Agreement or Compact with another State, or with a foreign Power, or engage in War, unless actually invaded, or in such imminent Danger as will not admit of delay (Art. I, Sec 10, cl. 3).

Appendix C: The Constitutional Line—The Constitutional Powers Reserved to the States[5]

These are merely some (not all) of the powers reserved to the States, listed for the public by advocates of the Constitution during the debates over ratification:
- Marriage
- Divorce
- Domestic relations
- Manufacturing (including labor relations)
- Business enterprises
- Agriculture
- Land use
- Land titles and conveyances
- Property outside of interstate trade
- Commerce wholly within state lines
- State and local governments
- Establishment and regulation of most crimes
- Civil litigation
- Social services, including care of the poor
- Training the militia and appointing militia officers
- Religion
- Education
- Roads (other than post roads)
- All other powers not delegated to the federal government

---

[5] Robert G. Natelson, The Original Constitution (2010); Natelson, The Enumerated Powers of States, 3 Nev. L.J. 469 (2002-2003).

Appendix D: Presidential Executive Order 12612 Regarding Federalism Issued by President Ronald Reagan

Presidential Executive Order 12612

(Note: President Reagan's effort to re-establish the proper role of the federal government through this Executive Order on Federalism was revoked in 1998 by Bill Clinton's new EO 13083, which largely re-justified the excessive unconstitutional role the federal government has assumed since the time of Franklin Roosevelt.)

Federalism

October 26, 1987

By the authority vested in me as President by the Constitution and laws of the United States of America, and in order to restore the division of governmental responsibilities between the national government and the States that was intended by the Framers of the Constitution and to ensure that the principles of federalism established by the Framers guide the Executive departments and agencies in the formulation and implementation of policies, it is hereby ordered as follows:

Section 1. Definitions. For purposes of this Order:

(a) "Policies that have federalism implications" refers to regulations, legislative comments or proposed legislation, and other policy statements or actions that have substantial direct effects on the States, on the relationship between the national government and the States, or on the distribution of power and responsibilities among the various levels of government.

(b) "State" or "States" refer to the States of the United States or America, individually or collectively, and, where relevant, to State governments, including units of local government and other political subdivisions established by the States.

Sec. 2. Fundamental Federalism Principles. In formulating and implementing policies that have federalism implications, Executive departments and agencies shall be guided by the following fundamental federalism principles:

(a) Federalism is rooted in the knowledge that our political liberties are best assured by limiting the size and scope of the national government.

(b) **The people of the States created the national government when they delegated to it those enumerated governmental powers** relating to matters beyond the competence of the individual States. **All other sovereign powers, save those expressly prohibited the States by the Constitution, are reserved to the States or to the people.**

(c) **The constitutional relationship among sovereign governments, State and national, is formalized in and protected by the Tenth Amendment to the Constitution.**

(d) The people of the States are free, subject only to restrictions in the Constitution itself or in constitutionally authorized Acts of Congress, to define the moral, political, and legal character of their lives.

(e) **In most areas of governmental concern, the States uniquely possess the constitutional authority, the resources, and the competence to discern the sentiments of the people and to govern accordingly.** In Thomas Jefferson's words, the States are "the most competent administrations for our domestic concerns and the surest bulwarks against antirepublican tendencies."

(f) The nature of our constitutional system encourages a healthy diversity in the public policies adopted by the people of the several States according to their own conditions, needs, and desires. In the search for enlightened public policy, individual States and communities are free to experiment with a variety of approaches to public issues.

(g) **Acts of the national government – whether legislative, executive, or judicial in nature – that exceed the enumerated powers of that government under the Constitution violate the principle of federalism established by the Framers.**

(h) Policies of the national government should recognize the responsibility of – and should encourage opportunities for – individuals, families, neighborhoods, local governments, and private associations to achieve their personal, social, and economic objectives through cooperative effort.

(i) **In the absence of clear constitutional or statutory authority, the presumption of sovereignty should rest with the individual States. Uncertainties regarding the legitimate authority of the national government should be resolved against regulation at the national level.**

Sec. 3. Federalism Policymaking Criteria. In addition to the fundamental federalism principles set forth in section 2, Executive departments and agencies shall adhere, to the extent permitted by law, to the following criteria when formulating and implementing policies that have federalism implications:

(a) There should be strict adherence to constitutional principles. Executive departments and agencies should closely examine the constitutional and statutory authority supporting any Federal action that would limit the policymaking discretion of the States, and should carefully assess the necessity for such action. To the extent practicable, the States should be consulted before any such action is implemented. Executive Order No. 12372 ("Intergovernmental Review of Federal Programs") remains in effect for the programs and activities to which it is applicable.

(b) **Federal action limiting the policymaking discretion of the States should be taken only where constitutional authority for the action is clear and certain and the national activity is necessitated by the presence of a problem of national scope.** For the purposes of this Order:

  (1) It is important to recognize the distinction between problems of national scope (which may justify Federal action) and problems that are merely common to the States (which will not justify Federal action because individual States, acting individually or together, can effectively deal with them).

  (2) **Constitutional authority for Federal action is clear and certain only when authority for the action may be found in a specific provision of the Constitution, there is no provision in the Constitution prohibiting Federal action, and the action does not encroach upon authority reserved to the States.**

(c) With respect to national policies administered by the States, the national government should grant the States the maximum administrative discretion possible. Intrusive, Federal oversight of State administration is neither necessary nor desirable.

(d) When undertaking to formulate and implement policies that have federalism implications, Executive departments and agencies shall:

  (1) Encourage States to develop their own policies to achieve program objectives and to work with appropriate officials in other States.

  (2) Refrain, to the maximum extent possible, from establishing uniform, national standards for programs and, when possible, defer to the States to establish standards.

(3) When national standards are required, consult with appropriate officials and organizations representing the States in developing those standards.

Sec. 4. Special Requirements for Preemption.

(a) To the extent permitted by law, Executive departments and agencies shall construe, in regulations and otherwise, a Federal statute to preempt State law only when the statute contains an express preemption provision or there is some other firm and palpable evidence compelling the conclusion that the Congress intended preemption of State law, or when the exercise of State authority directly conflicts with the exercise of Federal authority under the Federal statute.

(b) Where a Federal statute does not preempt State law (as addressed in subsection (a) of this section), Executive departments and agencies shall construe any authorization in the statute for the issuance of regulations as authorizing preemption of State law by rule-making only when the statute expressly authorizes issuance of preemptive regulations or there is some other firm and palpable evidence compelling the conclusion that the Congress intended to delegate to the department or agency the authority to issue regulations preempting State law.

(c) Any regulatory preemption of State law shall be restricted to the minimum level necessary to achieve the objectives of the statute pursuant to which the regulations are promulgated.

(d) As soon as an Executive department or agency foresees the possibility of a conflict between State law and Federally protected interests within its area of regulatory responsibility, the department or agency shall consult, to the extent practicable, with appropriate officials and organizations representing the States in an effort to avoid such a conflict.

(e) When an Executive department or agency proposes to act through adjudication or rule-making to preempt State law, the department or agency shall provide all affected States notice and an opportunity for appropriate participation in the proceedings.

Sec. 5. Special Requirements for Legislative Proposals. Executive departments and agencies shall not submit to the Congress legislation that would:

(a) Directly regulate the States in ways that would interfere with functions essential to the States' separate and independent existence or operate to directly displace the

States' freedom to structure integral operations in areas of traditional governmental functions;
(b) Attach to Federal grants conditions that are not directly related to the purpose of the grant; or
(c) Preempt State law, unless preemption is consistent with the fundamental federalism principles set forth in section 2, and unless a clearly legitimate national purpose, consistent with the federalism policymaking criteria set forth in section 3, cannot otherwise be met.

Sec. 6. Agency Implementation.

(a) The head of each Executive department and agency shall designate an official to be responsible for ensuring the implementation of this Order.
(b) In addition to whatever other actions the designated official may take to ensure implementation of this Order, the designated official shall determine which proposed policies have sufficient federalism implications to warrant the preparation of a Federalism Assessment. With respect to each such policy for which an affirmative determination is made, a Federalism Assessment, as described in subsection of this section, shall be prepared. The department or agency head shall consider any such Assessment in all decisions involved in promulgating and implementing the policy.
(c) Each Federalism Assessment shall accompany any submission concerning the policy that is made to the Office of Management and Budget pursuant to Executive Order No. 12291 or OMB Circular No. A-19, and shall:
  (1) Contain the designated official's certification that the policy has been assessed in light of the principles, criteria, and requirements stated in sections 2 through 5 of this Order;
  (2) Identify any provision or element of the policy that is inconsistent with the principles, criteria, and requirements stated in sections 2 through 5 of this Order;
  (3) Identify the extent to which the policy imposes additional costs or burdens on the States, including the likely source of funding for the States and the ability of the States to fulfill the purposes of the policy; and
  (4) Identify the extent to which the policy would affect the States' ability to discharge traditional State governmental functions, or other aspects of State sovereignty.

Sec. 7. Government-wide Federalism Coordination and Review.

(a) In implementing Executive Order Nos. 12291 and 12498 and OMB Circular No. A-19, the Office of Management and Budget, to the extent permitted by law and consistent with the provisions of those authorities, shall take action to ensure that the policies of the Executive departments and agencies are consistent with the principles, criteria, and requirements stated in sections 2 through 5 of this Order.

(b) In submissions to the Office of Management and Budget pursuant to Executive Order No. 12291 and OMB Circular No. A-19, Executive departments and agencies shall identify proposed regulatory and statutory provisions that have significant federalism implications and shall address any substantial federalism concerns. Where the departments or agencies deem it appropriate, substantial federalism concerns should also be addressed in notices of proposed rule-making and messages transmitting legislative proposals to the Congress.

Sec. 8. Judicial Review. This Order is intended only to improve the internal management of the Executive branch, and is not intended to create any right or benefit, substantive or procedural, enforceable at law by a party against the United States, its agencies, its officers, or any person.

RONALD REAGAN
THE WHITE HOUSE
October 26, 1987
Exec. Order No. 12612, 52 FR 41685, 1987 WL 181433 (Pres.)

(emphasis added)

APPENDIX E: SUMMARY OF UTAH HB76 FEDERAL LAW EVALUATION AND RESPONSE ACT (FLERA)

As outlined below, the Federal Law Evaluation and Response Act empowers state officers with a framework to honor and comply with their Article VI constitutional oath to stand as the "external check" to federal interference in the states' respective jurisdictions. The Federal Law Evaluation and Response Act:

1. Defines "federal law" as all:
   a. federal legislation;
   b. presidential executive orders; and
   c. all agency action, regulations or policies (UCA 63C-4-106(1));
2. Establishes plainly in Utah Code the "constitutional line," i.e. the constitutional standard for review and evaluation of all federal law, as only those powers expressly delegated by the Constitution to the federal government (UCA 63C-4-107);
3. Creates a Federalism Subcommittee of Utah's Constitutional Defense Council (UCA 63c-4-101(1-2), and (8));
4. Directs that the Federalism Subcommittee in applying the constitutional standard:
   a. Shall rely on the plain text of the Constitution (UCA 63C-4-107(3)(a)(i));
   b. Shall rely on the meaning of the text of the Constitution, as amended, at the time of its drafting and ratification (UCA 63C-4-107(3)(a)(ii));
   c. Shall rely on primary source documents directly relevant to, or created by a person directly involved in, the drafting, adoption, ratification, or initial implementation of the Constitution, as amended (UCA 63C-4-107(3)(a)(iii));
   d. May rely on other relevant sources, including federal court decisions (UCA 63C-4-107(3)(b)); and
   e. Is not bound by a holding of a federal court (UCA 63C-4-107(3)(c)).
5. Requires the Federalism Subcommittee to:
   a. Review and evaluate federal law (as broadly defined in the Act) against the above-mentioned "constitutional line" (UCA 63C-4-106(2) and 63C-4-107);
   b. Coordinate the review and evaluation of federal law directly with Utah's congressional delegation (UCA 63C-4-106(3) and (4));
   c. Coordinate the review and evaluation of federal law directly with a similarly

functioning council or legislative committee of other states (UCA 63C-4-106(4(c)) and (6), and UCA 63C-4-108);

d. Receive requests for review and evaluation through members of the CDC, which include: the Governor or Lt. Governor, the Utah Attorney General, President of the Utah Senate, Speaker of the Utah House, Minority Leaders of the Senate and House; the director of Utah's School and Institutional Trust Lands Administration (SITLA), and certain county commissioners or council members (UCA 63C-4-106(2));

e. Respond to federal law that crosses the "constitutional line" through the following:

   i. Provide written notice (*in concert with Utah's congressional delegation and other coordinating states*) to the offending federal branch or agency regarding how a particular federal law crosses the "constitutional line," formally requesting by a time certain the specific action the federal branch or agency intends to take to comply with the constitutional standard (UCA 63C-4-106(4)(b));

   ii. Failing satisfactory action through written notice, formally request the offending federal branch or agency receive a delegation of the Federalism Subcommittee (*in concert with Utah's congressional delegation and other coordinating states*) to mediate the issues of the federal action that crosses the "constitutional line" (UCA 63C-4-106(4)(c));

   iii. Request that the Governor call a special session of the legislature to address emergency consequences of federal law that crosses the "constitutional line" (UCA 63C-4-106(5));

   iv. Report twice a year to the Government Operations Committee the status of the CDC's and the Federalism Subcommittee's review, evaluation and response to federal law (UCA 63C-4-106(7)); and

   v. Report annually to every legislator the status of the review, evaluation and response to federal law for further action by the legislature as warranted by the official and public record developed by the CDC regarding all federal law that crosses the "constitutional line" (UCA 63C-4-102(9)).

INDEX

Alexander Hamilton, 4, 11, 17, 20, 21, 33, 34, 35, 39
Benjamin Franklin, 9, 34
Barriers, vii, 13, 14, 17, 18, 23, 30, 33, 38, 39
Bill Clinton, 30, 47
Bill of Rights, viii, 13, 24, 29, 30
Boston Massacre, 34
Checks and Balances, viii, 1, 2, 7, 13
Compound Republic, vii, viii, 1, 3, 4, 12, 13, 17, 18, 33, 34, 36, 37, 38
Consolidated Central Government, 10
Constitutional Line, vii, 13, 14, 17, 19, 23, 30, 33, 38, 39, 40, 45, 46, 53, 54
Continental Congress, 26, 34
Dallin H. Oaks, 11, 12
Despotism, 8, 18
Divide, Division, v, vii, viii, 4, 8, 11, 12, 17, 19, 30, 33, 36, 37, 47
Double Security, vii, 3, 4, 12, 33
Encroach, v, 4, 8, 17, 21, 35, 39, 49
Enumerated, 6, 15, 24, 26, 27, 46, 48
Executive Order, 30, 33, 47, 49, 51, 52, 53
External Controls, 2, 15, 29, 30, 31
Faults, viii, 19, 20, 30, 34, 35
Federal Law Evaluation and Response Act (FLERA), 33, 34, 53
Federal Reserve, 9
Federalism, 3, 19, 30, 36, 47, 48, 49, 51, 52, 53, 54
Few and Defined, 6, 7, 8, 28, 29, 41
Franklin D. Roosevelt, 37, 47
Fundamental Principles, vii, viii, 28
George Mason, viii
George Washington, viii, 2, 8, 11, 14, 28, 30
Government Powers, vii, 5, 48
Guardian, viii, 8, 13, 30, 33, 34
Indefinite, 6, 7, 25
Internal Controls, 2, 7, 30
James Jackson, 25
James Madison, vii, viii, 2, 4, 6, 7, 10, 11, 13, 20, 21, 25, 26, 29, 30, 33, 34, 35, 36

Index

James Wilson, 15
John Adams, 2, 5, 6, 16, 34
John Dickinson, viii, 20, 21, 30, 34, 35
Jurisdiction, vii, viii, 6, 18, 19, 20, 30, 34, 35, 36, 37, 38, 42, 44, 53
Legislative Devices, 20
Liberty, viii, 2, 5, 9, 10, 11, 12, 13, 17, 18, 19, 21, 30, 31, 33, 34, 35, 39
Limit, v, 4, 6, 8, 11, 12, 25, 26, 29, 30, 33, 34, 37, 41, 44, 48, 49
Line, v, vii, viii, 13, 14, 15, 16, 17, 19, 23, 30, 31, 33, 38, 39, 40, 42, 45, 46, 53, 54
Lord Acton, 1
Numerous and Indefinite, 6, 7
Oath, v, vii, 2, 13, 14, 43, 53
Original Meaning, 24, 27, 28
Over Passing, 4, 33, 34, 37
Patrick Henry, 6
Preemption, 50, 51
Resist, viii, 13, 21, 29, 30, 33, 35
Robert G. Natelson, v, 46
Ronald Reagan, 9, 30, 47-52
Samuel Adams, 18, 38, 39
Scott Matheson, 36
Self-evident, vii, 5, 20, 28
Separation of Powers, vii, 1, 3
Sovereign, viii, 11, 16, 17, 18, 19, 20, 21, 30, 34, 36, 37, 38, 48, 51
Tench Coxe, 26
Tenth Amendment, 11, 48
Thomas Hutchinson, 16
Thomas Jefferson, vii, 2, 3, 6, 8, 9, 10, 12, 14, 16, 17, 18, 23, 24, 25, 26, 27, 28, 29, 30, 33, 34, 38, 48
Thomas Paine, 31
Tyranny, 1, 19, 21
Unalienable Rights, vii, 5, 28, 34
Unlimited, 8, 10, 26
Usurpation, 4, 13, 28, 35
Vince Lombardi, 33
Where's the Line?, v, viii, 31, 40